The Path

Sqn Ldr Paridhei Singh (Retd.)

Chennai • Bangalore

CLEVER FOX PUBLISHING
Chennai, India

Published by CLEVER FOX PUBLISHING 2025
Copyright © Sqn Ldr Paridhei Singh 2025

All Rights Reserved.
ISBN: 978-93-67073-39-1

This book has been published with all reasonable efforts taken to make the material error-free after the consent of the author. No part of this book shall be used, reproduced in any manner whatsoever without written permission from the author, except in the case of brief quotations embodied in critical articles and reviews.

The Author of this book is solely responsible and liable for its content including but not limited to the views, representations, descriptions, statements, information, opinions and references ["Content"]. The Content of this book shall not constitute or be construed or deemed to reflect the opinion or expression of the Publisher or Editor. Neither the Publisher nor Editor endorse or approve the Content of this book or guarantee the reliability, accuracy or completeness of the Content published herein and do not make any representations or warranties of any kind, express or implied, including but not limited to the implied warranties of merchantability, fitness for a particular purpose. The Publisher and Editor shall not be liable whatsoever for any errors, omissions, whether such errors or omissions result from negligence, accident, or any other cause or claims for loss or damages of any kind, including without limitation, indirect or consequential loss or damage arising out of use, inability to use, or about the reliability, accuracy or sufficiency of the information contained in this book.

Humbly Offered to God Almighty and To My Gurus Mahaguruji Meiling and Grand Master Choa Kok Sui

who have got me where I am

Also to all the Gurus, from all over the world, from whom I have learnt

GREAT GURU LORD MAHAGURUJI MEILING

GREAT GURU GRAND MASTER CHO KOK SUI

Dedicated to My Mother Mrs Chandrakanta Mahajan

She was a poet too

She taught us how to live life by example . She was strong, courageous, bold, she made a path for herself, despite being a woman in a conservative society, she fought for her rights and stood by her ideals and her calling.

She was intelligent, creative, was into social service, did a lot for women upliftment and for the downtrodden, and was a very successful business woman.

She would read books, hear discourses of great philosophers, thinkers, saints and spiritual leaders and she introduced us to them. From a very early age we read books and live's of these great people.

She was spiritual and devoted. She prayed a lot and taught us to pray too.

She laid the foundation 🙏

We have a great example, to follow 🙏

Humbly Offered to God Almighty and To My Gurus Mahaguruji Meiling and Grand Master Choa Kok Sui

who have got me where I am 🙏

Also to all the Gurus, from all over the world, from whom I have learnt 🙏

GREAT GURU LORD MAHAGURUJI MEILING

GREAT GURU GRAND MASTER CHO KOK SUI

Dedicated to My Mother Mrs Chandrakanta Mahajan

She was a poet too

She taught us how to live life by example. She was strong, courageous, bold, she made a path for herself, despite being a woman in a conservative society, she fought for her rights and stood by her ideals and her calling.

She was intelligent, creative, was into social service, did a lot for women upliftment and for the downtrodden, and was a very successful business woman.

She would read books, hear discourses of great philosophers, thinkers, saints and spiritual leaders and she introduced us to them. From a very early age we read books and live's of these great people.

She was spiritual and devoted. She prayed a lot and taught us to pray too.

She laid the foundation 🙏

We have a great example, to follow 🙏

A Big Thank You to my friend and husband Group Capt C K Karthik for being such a great friend, always caring, helping, supporting and loving me unconditionally.

I wish to thank our son Surya and daughter Durga who are such evolved souls and are very matured people. So many times they share such valuable suggestions and advice which is valuable to both of us.

Super thankful to them for the unconditional love and respect and support they give me all the time. 💕❤️

A big thank you to our daughter Durga who does all the creative and art, behind my work. Pranic Healing sessions, meditations, talks, poetry, my previous book and this book too.

A BRIEF DESCRIPTION OF THE BOOK

These are a collection of musings which have dawned to my mind, when I asked questions to myself .

It is very rightly said that, all answers are within us, we only need to ask the right questions and we only need to, truly listen.

Write for myself, to help myself. Everyday I learn from these writings.

Thought everyone would benefit from them, therefore I'm sharing them.

Do not claim that I am perfect and have mastered them.

Am also just learning and am trying to get better and better everyday.

Would like to be identified as a student for life, on a lifelong learning experience and a traveller.

Hoping to just share this journey with all of you.

CONTENTS

1. About erring 1
2. Accept people as they are 3
3. All gurus are one 5
4. Awareness 8
5. Be detached 9
6. Be ready..11
7. Bless me o lord 13
8. Choices 15
9. Detachment is the key 17
10. Do things energetically first 19
11. Don't be the doer 21
12. Entitlement 24
13. Everything develops with a thought 27
14. Everything is a training 29
15. Feelings 32
16. Fly higher 35
17. Give give give 37
18. God give a mother like mine to everyone 39
19. Good angle bad angle 42
20. Gravest danger 44
21. Have you tried the smile? 47
22. How aware we are 49
23. How little we know 51
24. How much do we know ourselves.............................53
25. I am a child of god 55
26. I am a learner for life 58
27. I want this i want that..60
28. If you're sad 63
29. In love with camp fires...65

30.	Inner reflection 68
31.	It is perfect the way it is 70
32.	It's all about doing the right action 72
33.	It's all in the mind 75
34.	It's me 77
35.	Jealousy 80
36.	Just try it 84
37.	Keep positive 86
38.	Leave behind 90
39.	Leave the movie behind 94
40.	Let's keep our inner happiness 97
41.	Let's wish other people well 99
42.	Look 102
43.	Look where we have reached 104
44.	Love yourself do good work 106
45.	Manifestation 111
46.	Mastering oneself 114
47.	May my will match 116
48.	May peace be with us 118
49.	Meditate 120
50.	Meditate 122
51.	My limitations 124
52.	My prayers my blessings today 🙏 🖤 126
53.	Negative thoughts 129
54.	Negativity 132
55.	No life like a life being an instrument of the guru 134
56.	Nothing is beyond ourselves 137
57.	Only all about us 140
58.	Only when we 145
59.	Our inner self 147
60.	Our secret desire: perfection 149
61.	Our true inner self 151
62.	Peace 153
63.	Peace inside 157

64.	Perceptions	159
65.	Perfect ourselves	161
66.	Persistence	165
67.	Positive thoughts	168
68.	Pray for wisdom	170
69.	Problems	172
70.	Seek the divine	175
71.	Self-discovery	178
72.	Stand tall	181
73.	Stop	183
74.	That one thought	185
75.	The pitfalls of the negative	189
76.	The quest for happiness	192
77.	The secret is ….	195
78.	Think what you want	198
79.	Thoughts control	200
80.	Time	202
81.	To be happy for others	205
82.	Universe inside us	208
83.	Want peace?	212
84.	Watch out	215
85.	Watch what you send out	218
86.	We all know	219
87.	We are a small speck	222
88.	We are perfect the way we are	224
89.	We can be happy anywhere	226
90.	We do so much	229
91.	We have a choice	231
92.	We have all the power	233
93.	We have to be convinced	235
94.	We will need	238
95.	What are we looking for	240
96.	What we think we become	243
97.	When i will	247

98. Who am i to judge you?	251
99. Wholesome thoughts	253
100. Why are we here?	256
101. With a thought	259
Bio	*261*

1

ABOUT ERRING

Sometimes we err
Maybe knowingly
But a lot of times
Unknowingly

If we had control
At that moment
If we had wisdom
We certainly wouldn't err

We must never
Blame ourselves
Feel guilty
Be harsh on our self

Remember it's
Just about how
Evolved we are
How aware we are

Don't give attention
To the fault
Just forgive yourself
And keep moving

The Path

The more we give
Energy to the mistake
The more it
Will grow

Just concentrate
On our self growth
Self awareness
Self development

As we grow
Slowly gradually
Our mistakes
Will reduce

The learning
Is important
The growth
Is important

The evolution
Of our soul
Is important
Just one mistake isn't

Let's go ahead
With our work
Courageously
Confidently

And be the humans
The soul
The perfection
We desire to be

Paridhei 🙏 ♥

ACCEPT PEOPLE AS THEY ARE

One key to happiness
Amongst the chaos of life
Is to accept people
Just the way they are

No expectations no desire
For them to change
No criticism no hatred
For what they are

Just a silent soft
Acceptance of it all
People will be just
What they choose to be

They don't need to
Fit into any mould
That we deem fit
That is according to us

We are not perfect
Why expect anyone else to be
We have our limitations
Others will have theirs

Also, what seems right to us
Maybe flawed too
As our judgements
Are based on our wisdom

And our wisdom
Is limited is defective too
Our inferences our conclusions
All have limitations

Just let people be
Just ignore the faults
Stay in the safe haven
Of your own consciousness

If you don't get along
Just keep distance
And without criticism
With an acceptance, withdraw

No negativity but stay safe
Keep to your own
Accept don't expect
And watch them at a distance

Never let your positivity
Your happiness
And peace get affected
By what you see in others

That's the safe peaceful
Way to be
The best way to be
The key happiness

Paridhei 🙏 🖤

3

ALL GURUS ARE ONE

It's time
We understand
We realise
That all gurus are one
In their mission

They only intend
For the evolution
Of humanity
To dispel
The darkness
To serve
To create harmony
And peace
On earth
And this universe

They mean the
Best
Not only
To humankind
But also
To mother nature
To mother earth
To animal kingdom
To our environment

They choose
Different paths
Different ways to serve
Device variety of work
Open different schools
Based on their choices
Their strengths
Maybe from different
Religions

But they are all united
They're working together
In the inner world

When good work is done
Anywhere in any school
They all rejoice

When any soul evolves
When humanity evolves
Anywhere in any school
They all join together
To bless

When anyone is stuck
In any school
In any work
They have no differentiation
They help, they assist
They offer cooperation

They love and respect
Each other
Each other's work
Each other's school

If your intention is pure
If you're on the path
You can ask help
From anyone of them
You'll surely receive help

When our gurus are one
Then why have
The difference in our minds
Why not respect, love
Appreciate
Offer help
To all
From all schools

Paridhei 🙏 🖤

4

AWARENESS

Awareness that these
Feelings exist

Knowing that they
Are not positive

Not good for me
Not good for my health

Not good for my
Mind body and soul

Control
For keeping them at bay

Will
For discarding them

Action
For changing them to
Something positive

Result
Peace and happiness 😊

5

BE DETACHED

We can end the suffering
Our own misery
By our mind, our thoughts our positivity

But what about the suffering
Of other people?
Of the world ?

What if that disturbs us
We feel bad and sad
For the distress of others

How to put an end
To the suffering of the world
War, poverty, disease, calamity

How can we stay happy
When the world around us
Is paining, is devastated

Especially our near and dear ones
Our loved ones
Our friends and family

Attachment to other's sadness
Should also be avoided
We can feel for them, but not dwell

We can pray, bless, heal
We can do acts of kindness
We can try to ease out the pains

But be detached
Do whatever we can
But ourselves stay peaceful and happy

Within ourselves
Let no turmoil develop
Let there be no upheavals

All is maya, just know that
And everyone is affected
In the measure of their karma

Also everything is impermanent
This world and so is the suffering
Us and so also our vicissitudes

Empathise, be compassionate
Help and heal
But stay in your peace

Nothing should be able to
Disturb our peace and happiness
That's the key

This, our bearing our demeanour
Will help the world
Be a better place

A pranic healer's point of view

Paridhei 

6

BE READY

First
Be ready to stay away
From mental chatter
Be ready to stir clear
Of internal noise
Be ready to break free
Of our thoughts
Keep them at bay

When we're wanting to
Soar higher
Touch higher levels of consciousness

We really have to
Get past these
To free ourselves

They bring us down
Pull us down
With their weight

And the negative ones
They'll get us down
Even more
They shake us more
They stick more
Very difficult to
Break through

We can't get anywhere
Without first dealing
With all of these

So let's not
Just let it be
Let's deal with them

Let's be
Aware of them
Observe them
Handle them
Steer clear of them

And be free

And soar higher

Paridhei 🙏 🖤

7

BLESS ME O LORD

God almighty always give me
The right knowledge
The correct interpretation
Of what's happening
In the material world
And the inner world

May i not have erroneous
Judgements and impressions
Protect me from
Misconceptions, delusions
Illusions of all kinds
May i see, know the truth

No matter what the chaos
In the middle of the turmoil
May the truth reveal itself to me
May i know the facts correctly
And my judgements
Be based on this truth

Knowing and learning
This truth, the real facts
This is the first step, then
May i have the correct inferences
May i know the apt answers
May i understand properly

The Path

Then may i act unerringly
Knowing the truth
And the accurate meaning
May my actions be guided
In a way to generate
The least negative karma

Guide me o god
To the correct path
May i know where to go
Without being lost
May i approach closer
To you in every step

Bless me o god 🙏🩶🤍

Paridhei 🙏🩶

8

CHOICES

Everyday we are making choices
We are choosing some steps
Over others to shape our life
We are choosing some reactions
Over others as responses
We are choosing some people
Over others to be with
We are choosing some professions
Over others as our vocations
We are choosing some hobbies
Over others as our time pass
We are choosing to spend on somethings
Over other expenses

Our life is an outcome
Of our choices
Our world is built
On our choices

So in order to live
A happy fulfilling life
We have to make
The proper choices

To make proper choices
We will need sharp wisdom
And deeper understanding

These need to be
Gradually developed
Worked on
Toiled hard on
Persistently pursued
Improved upon
Mastered

Meditation helps
Get that clarity of thought
That critical thinking
That decision making
So that we make good decisions
And correct choices

Let's meditate regularly

Paridhei 🙏 🖤

9

DETACHMENT IS THE KEY

Detach yourself
Detach yourself from your
Thoughts
Watch them from far

Detach yourself from your
Emotions
They are not you, they don't
Define you

Detach yourself from the
Happenings
Move out of the involvement

Detach yourself from the
Situations
Observe them as a stranger

Observe watch objectively
Stay detached
Keep yourself away

Detachment is a means
To better control
Of yourself
And everything around

Carry on with your work,
Life and it's happenings
Being detached

Detachment is the key
To success

Paridhei 🙏 ♥

10

DO THINGS ENERGETICALLY FIRST

Do things energetically first
Results will be faster

Energy follows thought
Give thought and energy to an intention

We are doing it unknowingly
All the time

We think a thought before any act
We first give the thought the energy

Do it consciously now on
Give it the thought, the energy

Give it all the positivity
Imagine you are altering things energetically

Then act, then do things
You will be surprised by the results

Everything is energy
And energy is everything

Send positive energy first
To all that you want to achieve

Watch the results be positive
The success and the growth excel

Health wealth success abundance
Everything is better with the right energy

We are all energy beings 🙏 ♥

Paridhei 🙏 ♥

A pranic healer's point of view

As taught by my guru master choa
So many techniques are taught to us to energetically do and change things in pranic healing.

Super thankful to the guru for the amazing yet simple teachings 🙏 ♥

11

DON'T BE THE DOER

Watch it!
All is a maya
All is an illusion
Just be detached
Just watch from far
Don't get entangled
Don't get confused
Don't get harassed
Don't panic

A situation is
Challenging
Only because
We are attached to
To an outcome
That we want
We want it
Our way
Or no way

Wait wait wait
Let it go
Let it all
Settle down
Let the solutions
Appear on their own

Let the mystery
Reveal itself
Let the gift materialise

Be steadfast in
Your inner self
Peaceful calm
Happy cheerful
Watch everything
Don't get hassled
Don't get stressed
Don't be nervous
Don't be perturbed

Everything will
Sort out on its own
Don't be the doer
Leave it to the
Supreme power
God almighty
Universe
The guru
The great great ones

Let them do it
Through you
Let them guide you
Take you by hand
Through the jungle
Of illusion
Intertwined jumbled
Thoughts dreams
Reality, myriad of choices

Let them take you
To the right path
The correct way
For you
Let them guide you
Let them clear
Everything up
For you
The way they want

Just be detached
From any outcome
That you desire
And accept the
Consequences
They have for you
That's truly for you
That will be good
For you and the situation

Have faith
No matter what
They are taking
Care of you
And mean
The best for you
Though it may
Not seem like that
Right now

But that is the truth
They have your back
They are in your favour

Paridhei

12

ENTITLEMENT

We want to have,
We yearn for
An abundant life

We will get only
That much as
We are karmically entitled

We want to have,
We yearn for
A successful career

We will get only
That much as
We are karmically entitled

We want to have,
We yearn for
A lot of prosperity

We will get only
That much as
We are karmically entitled

We want to have,
We yearn for
Lots of love and affection

We will get only
That much as
We are karmically entitled

We want to have,
We yearn for
Absolute good health and fitness

We will get only
That much as
We are karmically entitled

We want to have,
We yearn for
Great spiritual growth

We will get only
That much as
We are karmically entitled

We want to have,
We yearn for
Guidance

We will get only
That much as
We are karmically entitled

We want to have,
We yearn for
A great spiritual guru

We will get only
That much as
We are karmically entitled

Even if, we want to have,
We yearn for
Just positive thoughts and emotions

We will get only
That much as
We are karmically entitled

So, we see the need to
Increase our karmic entitlement
How do we do it?

Service, service, service
Be of service to humanity
In some form or other

Giving, giving, giving,
Give and share
Whatever you have to all around

Pray, pray, pray
Pray to god almighty
To guide, to show the path

Serve, give, pray
For a greater entitlement
For a wonderful abundant life.

Paridhei 🙏 ♥

13

EVERYTHING DEVELOPS WITH A THOUGHT

Everything develops
With a thought

Everything starts
With a strong will

Everything begins
With a firm resolve

Everything will elaborate
On our vision

It's all in the mind
It all starts there

The stronger our thought
Our will, our resolve

The faster we will
Reach our goals

The faster we will
Manifest our dreams

So, it all depends
On the strength of these

But, if there's chaos, turmoil,
Negativity in the mind

Will we be able to
Produce strong thoughts?

Will we be able to get the
Razor sharp thinking?

Will we get the clarity?
Will we get the answers?

Here, we see the need to purify
Our minds and thoughts

We see need to steer clear
Of negative thoughts

It's pertinent to introspect
It's important to purify

Only pure and positive thoughts,
Emotions and feelings

Will lead us to success
Will reach us to our goals

Will take us to greater heights
Will bring us to happiness

Paridhei 🙏 ♥

14

EVERYTHING IS A TRAINING

Don't get flustered
Don't be perturbed
Don't be agitated
Don't get upset

At the situation
At hand
At the circumstances
Not so favourable

Everything is a
Training
Everything is
Preparing you

For a future
More secure
A better beautiful
Tomorrow

Take the training
To be more prepared
To face life's challenges
And vagaries fearlessly

This readiness
Will help you
Take on life
And make it better

Be steadfast
Be undeterred
Be determined
Be committed

Concentrate
On the lesson
On gaining
The experience

Learn from others
From everyone
Around you
Don't miss the chance

Friends will teach us
But don't let the
Adversaries go
Without the lesson

Make sure you learn
From whatever
Life hurls at you
Whatever the situation

Make adversity
Your friend
See it in the eye
Embrace it

And take the
Opportunity to
Learn and grow
To master life

Continue to evolve
Become a better
Version
Of yourselves

A person with
A growth mindset
Who is continually
Learning

Will never fail
Will never lose
Will never succumb
To defeat

So keep your wits
About you in life
And be ever ready
To be a good student

Master the art of life

Paridhei 🙏 🖤

15

FEELINGS

It's not only
Our thoughts
We have to be
Careful about

We have to
Take care
Of our feelings
Observe them
Watch them
Control them

These feelings
Crop up
Change the
Entire scenario

They will
Colour our thoughts
And then actions
With whatever colour
They possess

They affect everything

Through the glasses
Of feelings
We will see
The world
In the same colour

Feeling sad
Feeling angry
Feeling depressed
Feeling upset
Feeling hurt

Whatever the feeling
We will feel
Thoughts in the same
Frequency
And then our
Actions will also
Show the same

Watch your feelings
Switch them
Change them
If need be

Feel happy
Feel excited
Feel good
Feel content
Feel peaceful

Get into a more
Positive mindset
Then think
Then act

To know
What our feelings are
We need awareness
Take the help
Of meditation

To switch
To control
We need
Inner strength
Take the help
Of meditation

Command our
Feelings
Take charge of our
Thoughts
Control our actions

To live
A more positive
Happy peaceful
And joyful
Life

Paridhei 🙏 🖤

16

FLY HIGHER

We are not our thoughts
To experience supreme bliss
Unison with the higher self
We have to move above
The mind and the thoughts

That's the difficult part to do
We get entangled with our mind
Our thoughts form a web
Which trap us into them
We find it difficult to break free

And if we have negative thoughts
They have a sticky nature
They are clingy, they stick to us
Much more than positivity
Much more than peaceful thoughts

So, first we have
To keep our thoughts
Peaceful calm and positive
Keep them clear
Keep them placid

Most of us are
Most of the times
Just fighting
Our thoughts our emotions
We are unable to move up

There is so much more
To us, than our thoughts
Even than our body
We are not our mind
We will need to break free

To fly into higher realms
To achieve oneness with
Our higher soul
To be connected to the
Divine and pure

We need to keep
Our thoughts pure
So that we can easily
Soar in the inner world
Achieve higher consciousness
Be free

Paridhei 🙏 🖤

17

GIVE GIVE GIVE

The trick to
Abundance
In each and every
Sphere of
One's life

Is to give away
More and more
Of what you want
In your life
Just give give give

Want love ?
Spread love
All around
Send out
Loving vibes

Genuinely give
Love to everyone
Around you
Let them
Be loved and cared for

Want to be
Healed ?
Help others heal
Spread wellness
And healthcare

Want to be
Happy ?
Ooze out joy
Make others happy
Gift people smiles

Want to be
Wealthy ?
Have prosp
Give give give
Share share share

Share with others
All that you have
You will get in
Return more of
What you want

Whatever we give
Comes back to us
Multiplied
Many many times
The key is in giving

Paridhei 🙏 🖤

18

GOD GIVE A MOTHER LIKE MINE TO EVERYONE

God give a mother
Like mine to everyone

May everyone be
Blessed with such

Kind of love care
And support 💗

An epitome of love
Sacrifice and devotion

To us her children
And our lives

She gave so much
Much more than

Was normally possible
Or what was available

She never thought of
Her own self

Her likes and dislikes
Her wants and desires

Always kept her
Children above everything

She would know
What each child wants

Even before we could
Express or speak it

With her love and support
Each one of us blossomed

To the best of our ability
To the best possible versions

We owe so much of us
What we are and what we have

So much of our character
So much of our personality

So much of our success
So much of ourselves

To her and her hard work
Sincerity and dedication to us

We are really lucky
To have a mom like her

Words cannot express
The gratitude i feel

For the blessing of a
Mom like mine

God give a mother
Like mine to everyone

Paridhei 🙏 🖤

19

GOOD ANGLE BAD ANGLE

There's a good angle
To something

And a bad angle
To the same thing too

There will be pros and cons
To everything

There will be good qualities
In some people

There will be bad qualities
Also in the same people

While we are busy
Scrutinising the faults of something

Someone somewhere
Is building on the positives

Creating more rights
Rather than the wrongs

Seeing the good
And ignoring the bad in someone

Making life long friendships
Having healthy, happy relationships

Working hard on the positives
Building business empires

Mending the problems
Finding solutions and solving

If we just find the negatives
And don't bother to look for positives

We are sure shot heading
For failure

In whatever we are doing
Wherever we are

Converting the adverse
To something favourable

Is what the successful do
What they use for victory

Whatever it is that we're facing
Building on positives is the way

Paridhei 🙏 🖤

GRAVEST DANGER

To get a chance to
Improve ourselves
In this lifetime
Is the greatest gift
We could ever
Get from almighty

What greater danger
God, guru can protect
Us form
Other than our
Own follies
Own errors

What better protection
Than from ourselves
And the mistakes
We make
Hurt ourselves with
Forever and ever

Infact that's the only
Thing that can
Hurt us gravely,
Us ourselves!
No other enemy
Like us ourselves

What better awakening
Than to our own faults
It's a gift to be able
To see our foolishness or
We could go through life
Being completely ignorant

Let's be truly grateful
For the opportunities
To remove all faults
To better ourselves
To relive our life
With refining ourselves

A chance for a new life
Regenerated with
A new improved us
And continuous
Rejuvenation with
Self enhancement

This is the true gift
As there is no sign
Of life like that,
Of growth!
All living things grow
That's the true sign

True indication
That we're alive,
This inner development!
True sign that we
Will surely have a
Better life than earlier

The only way to
A finer life
Is through this self love
Love for improvement
Let's be thankful
For a chance to better life

Nothing more
Precious than
Learning and growth
I'm truly grateful for
All the learning
And chance to excel myself

Thank you to god and guru for this gift 💗 🙏
💚

Paridhei 🙏💚

21

HAVE YOU TRIED THE SMILE?

When troubles surround you
Just try the smile
You'll surely find them easy

When you're down and out
Just try the smile
You'll surely be uplifted

When your chips are down
Just try the smile
You'll surely find a way out

When you feel sad or lonely
Just try the smile
You'll surely feel better

When you feel angry or irritated
Just try the smile
You'll surely be calmed down

When you feel frustrated and agitated
Just try the smile
You'll surely feel finer

No matter what's happening
Around you
Inside you
Just try the smile
The world will spontaneously
Suddenly
Get brighter and better

Smile for no reason
Smile for no purpose
Just try the smile

Paridhei 🙏 🖤

22

HOW AWARE WE ARE

These fears, tensions,
Stressful thoughts
We have
Will ease out

These internal uproars
Will soon subside
All the worry, the anxiety
Will vanish finally

But how fast they will,
Will depend on
How aware we are
How conscious we are

We just need to be
Aware of them
We just need to
Witness them

We need not
Abhor them
We must not
Resist them

If we simply
Accept them
If we don't
Judge them

Just let them be
With awareness
With consciousness
Watch them

Watch them
Cause the upheaval
Then watch them
Slowly subside

They will soon
Subside
They will quickly
Disappear

But how fast they will
Will depend on
How aware we are
How conscious we are

Paridhei 🙏 🖤

23

HOW LITTLE WE KNOW

It's surprising how little we know
The knowledge is so vast
And our knowledge of it tiny winy
All the information
In all the libraries
Even in google
So much, yet so little
Compared to the vastness
Of true pure knowledge

We work, we slumber
Burn the midnight oil
Yet we will know only a little
We may think we know a lot
But there's a lot more

All our notions, our impressions
Our decisions are based
On this little information.
So naive, so inadequate
So inappropriate
Ignorance clouds our minds

That's why i pray 🙏
I pray to god almighty 🙏
To the all knowing 🙏
And to the great guru 🙏

To guide us
To show us the way
To hold our hand
Take us through life
With ease, with love
Divinely affect our impressions
Out judgements
Help us take correct decisions
Keep us protected
We may never be lost
Help us live a blessed life

Guide us o lord 🙏 ♥
Bless us o lord 🙏 ♥
Protect us o lord 🙏 ♥

Paridhei

24

HOW MUCH DO WE KNOW OURSELVES

The thing is how much
 Do we know ourselves

Our positives our negatives
Our strengths and weaknesses

To know our weaknesses
We will need awareness

High degree of awareness
Higher level of truly knowing ourselves

Every time we feel we know our negatives
We work on them
And with awareness we see
Few more crop up

This awareness comes from
Meditation and regular

Self introspection

And remember these negative qualities we have
Will be hindrances to any thing we want to do
Maybe spiritual or material

We need to get rid of these
Let's meditate regularly

Paridhei 🙏 ♥

25

I AM A CHILD OF GOD

Say it frequently
I am a child of god
I am a gift of god
To the world

Just watch
How
This statement
Changes us
How
The responsibility
Comes to us
How we alter
Our behaviour
How we value
Ourselves more
How we value
Our time more
How what we do
Becomes important
Even our mundane
Tasks and work
How we become
More careful
How we train
Ourselves

How we will
Live upto
This

As we are
A gift of god
Then we have
A higher purpose
A deeper meaning
To life

We have so
Much to do

No matter where
We are placed
What profession
Or vocation we have
What are our
Talents and strengths

We have the power
To do more
Be more
Give more

We can spread
Love
Happiness
Joy
Affection
Healing
Wisdom
Peace
Goodness
Everywhere

Remember
We are god's gift
To the world
Repeat it every day

Remember
We are important
What we do
Is important
And every little bit
Counts

Paridhei 🙏 🖤

26

I AM A LEARNER FOR LIFE

I am a learner for life
I have pledged to be so

What better learning
Than about our selves

What better to know
Than knowing ourselves

It is the most difficult
But the most important

Without knowing ourselves
We will err
Wherever we are
Whatever
 We're doing

We'll never be able
To succeed
If we don't learn
About ourselves

Knowing
Our positives
Our negatives
What to improve
How to improve
These will take us
A long way

Knowing and learning
How to be better
Than before
Will take us to the top
In whatever game we play

Life is learning
We learn from
The day we are born

And we learn even today
We better learn

I am a learner for life
I have pledged to be so

Paridhei 🙏 🖤 ♡

27

I WANT THIS
I WANT THAT

I want this
I want that

This should be like this
This should be like that

I desire this
I yearn that

I detest this
I reject that

Everyone should follow
My instructions, my ideas

Life should be
According to what i perceive

This is how we push
This is what we wish

But we ourselves
Don't know anything

Where these desires
Are coming from

Where are our urges
Controlled from

What is the basis of
Our likes and dislikes

We want to propel
Life in a certain direction

With constricted view
With limited knowledge

That's why the confusion
That's why the chaos

Leave all control
Leave all domination

Act in a way we feel like
But know that we are ignorant

Take decisions, walk the path
But be aware we don't know much

We don't know the entire situation
We can't see too far

So if outcomes
Are sometimes

Not as desired
Not as planned

Just be cheerful
Still

The supreme almighty
Knows everything

Will give us what we need
May not be what we want

Don't control with our desires
Let life flow effortlessly

What's best for us
Will come to us

What is not good for us
Will not come to us

Base our attitude
On this confidence

Teach our ignorant self
To let go of command

The supreme being
Is taking care of me

This is the belief
To have

This is the basis
Of happiness and cheer

Paridhei 🙏 ♥

28

IF YOU'RE SAD

If you're sad
Try to live
A purposeful life
You will be uplifted
When you lift others

If you're not satisfied
With what life
Has to offer you
Live a meaningful life
No satisfaction better

If you're not happy
With the outcomes
Of your actions and deeds
Live a mindful life
Be aware of every moment

If you feel lack
Of anything
Love, happiness, money
Give that away
Spread and share what you seek

If you feel sick
Fall ill regularly
Look at your thoughts
Negativity and stress
Settle in your body

Finally one will
Find peace and happiness
Only in positivity
Only in living a
Meaningful
Purposeful
Mindful life

Paridhei 🙏 🖤

29

IN LOVE WITH CAMP FIRES

When we sit around a camp fire
Watching the embers
In the darkness
Just enjoying the singing
Basking in the moonlight
Gazing at the stars
Talking with each other
Listening to jokes
Just this and nothing else
On our mind

We realise how much
Of a waste of time
It is to live the hectic life
We live
Running around after
This goal, that ambition
Mindlessly and aggressively
Pursuing the future
Or else seeking entertainment
And enjoyment
Thirsting fun and pleasure
In the malls, dazzling parties
Discos, pubs and bars

When all we need
Is this setting in life
Just a soft spot
To sit and relax
Leave everything
And just be
When all you can do is
Stare in the darkness
Or lie down
And look up at the sky
The beauty of this universe
Enfolding in front of you

Ofcourse
We can't all leave our lives
But we can frequently
Camp in mother nature
Under the sky
Near forest covers
Close to the rivers
And feel refreshed
Like nothing else can
Make us feel
Feel one with the universe
And feel empowered
Without doing anything
Much achieved
In the material world

These frequent breaks
Are much required
Because mother nature
Is the best healer
The sound of rivers
Running by
Will be sound healing

The fresh air
Can clear any pollution
That's been in our lungs
And the skies and stars
Will bring peace
In any turmoil or chaos

This is much required
Let's do this often 🩷

Paridhei 🙏 🩷

Dedicated to all my friends who run adventure and outdoor companies, working hard and have dedicated themselves to it. They continue to serve us " the outdoors "and light camp fires for us and make living with mother nature accessible for us.

30

INNER REFLECTION

When i started reflecting
When i started retrospecting

When i started looking
For negative thoughts

I found so many
Some totally unknown

Some i wasn't
Even aware of

Some in such areas of life
Which i never thought of

So so many
It was unbelievable

I always thought
Of myself being positive

Where were these
Buried ?

When i started changing
These

Started
Thinking positive thoughts

I found so many
Of them, needed the change

Then i realised
The importance of reviewing

Our inner self
Every now and then

As frequently
As possible

Maybe even every time
All the time

Contemplate ruminate
Mull

Don't let a single
Negative thought pass

We can never stop
The introspection

As it's a continuing process
We never know when, where

The negative
Sets in

Paridhei

31

IT IS PERFECT THE WAY IT IS

Sometimes we just need
To tell ourselves
Whatever is happening
Is for the best for me

It may be difficult
To see the ways
Of god almighty
At the moment

Things may not be
Going as planned
We may doubt
The circumstances

Situation might seem
Going against us now
The outcomes may look
Adverse to what we expect

But believe it or not
It is perfect
All is occurring
For the best for us

No matter what we loose
No matter what we gain
Faith that it's for the best
Is what we need to have

Relax and enjoy
The ride even if bumpy
Because that's what
It is meant to be

We need to believe
We need to have trust
In the supreme being
In god almighty

That only what's
Good for us
Will come to us
The best possible

The greatest good
Is transpiring
Everything is perfect
As it ought to be

Paridhei 🙏 ♥

32

IT'S ALL ABOUT DOING
THE RIGHT ACTION

It's all about doing
The right action

It's the difficult part too

Every action takes us
Miles away from
An alternate destination

Even a small action
Matters

For all of it to fall
In place
Firstly we need
To know our
Correct destination

We must aim correctly
We must know
Our likes dislikes
Our ambitions
Our capabilities
Our strengths

And then formulate
Our goals

How will we know this ?
Only through awareness

We must then know
The right actions
That will take us there
An incorrect act can take
Us far away

How will we know this ?
Only through awareness

That's why we must
Pray and meditate

Pray so that we
Get divine guidance
And know correctly
What's the best goal
For us
What's the best action
For us

Meditate so that we
Develop intuition
And awareness
To know our goal
And know how
To reach it
And to know
When and where
We're going wrong

So that
We know where to go
What to do
And do the
Correct actions.

Paridhei 🙏 ♥

33

IT'S ALL IN THE MIND

It's all in the mind
Our diseases
Our luck
Our situations
Favourable or
Unfavourable

All depend
On what we
Have thought
About them
In our mind
In our inner world

Think health
Think healing
Think success
Think positive
Think abundance
Think love

Sow these seeds
In our inner world
Into the subconscious
That's what
We will harvest
We will receive

If we think
We have
Good health
That's what
We will have
We will manifest

If we think
We have
Abundance
That's what
We will have
We will manifest

If we think
We have love
That's what
We will have
We will manifest

What we believe
Will happen
So better
To keep our
Thoughts positive
And our mind pure

Stay positive
Stay diligent
Stay judicious
Watch our thoughts
Be careful
Accept only positive

Paridhei 🙏 🖤

34

IT'S ME

God i can
Take care of
Everything else
Teach me how to
Handle myself.

My thoughts
My emotions
My feelings
Guide me
To be in control

I know for sure
It's not there
Outside somewhere
It in here
Within me

It's not
That person
That situation
That event
That circumstance

It's all me
I myself
I am responsible
It's my doing
It's my own creation

Let this awareness
Always be with me
Never should i
Be in an illusion
That outside
Is in control

With this awareness
Let me be in charge
Let me be in control
Let me change
What's required

I am creating
I will create
I am deciding
I will decide
What world i am in

This world
Around me
I have made
It's my creation
I am responsible

It's me
To praise
Or to blame
To alter
Or to change

It's me

Paridhei 🙏 🖤

35

JEALOUSY

We ruin so much
Of our own happiness
By jealousy

Our problem is
If we want something
Really bad

We may even get it
We may even achieve it
We may even m manifest it

But we sometimes don't
Want others to have
What they want

It occasionally upsets us
When we see others
Get what they want

We now and then
Want others
Not to achieve success

So instead
Of being happy
For what we achieve

We're busy being
Unhappy
For what others achieve

What an unnecessary
Unfortunate misery
This is

Comparing competing
With others
Is such a futile action

It never leaves us
With peace
And contentment

Happiness is of
Utmost importance
It's imperative for life

When we could be
Happy and grateful
For all that we have

Why should we
Invite unhappiness
And suffering

For no purpose
No rhyme or reason!
Needless anguish!

Being happy
For others and their
Success and achievement

Is the key to being
Happy ourselves
And end distress

Wish for the best
For ourselves
And for others

Wish for success
For ourselves
And for others

Will bring us
Immense happiness
And contentment

It will attract
More abundance
More success to us

More than
We can ever think of
We can fathom

The universe gives
Open heartedly
And unconditionally

To those who give
And wish the best
For others

So let's be happy
For others, their success
And their achievements

To find true happiness
Within ourselves
Uninterrupted, unadulterated

Count our own blessings
And be full of gratitude
For what we have today

Paridhei 🙏 🤍

36

JUST TRY IT

Just try it
Just try it

Replace negative
With positive

And see how
Refreshing it is

Replace jealousy
With wishing others well

Replace revenge
With forgiveness

Replace hatered and dislike
With tolerance

Let there be neutrality
If not strong love

Replace anger
With patience and peace

Replace resentment
With understanding

Replace fear
With faith

Replace ego
With selflessness

Replace pride
With humility

Just try it
And see how liberating it is

Just try it
And feel truly happy

No amount of
Material gratification

Can give us peace
And satisfaction

Like when we
Make ourselves positive

When we purify ourselves
When we improve ourselves

Happiness is unbound
When we work on ourselves

That is the way to take
That is the path to tread on

Just try it
Just try it out

Paridhei

37

KEEP POSITIVE

Whenever we have
Disagreements

Whenever we have
Heated arguments

Whenever we have
Discord

Whenever we have
Negativity brewing

Whenever we have
Animosity

Whenever we have
Hatered

With people around us
With our colleagues

With our family
With our friends

We have to always
Remember

They are not perfect
Accept them the way they are

But most importantly
We are not perfect

Our opinion might
Be biased

We are limited by our
Restricted understanding

We have our short comings
They have theirs

We don't like
Somethings in others

Other people will not like
Somethings in us

Something in them irks us
Something in us irks them too

Just like we're learning
They are also growing

Treat people like people
Not like enemies

Do not respond
To negativity with negativity

Always be peaceful
And send out positive vibes

Negative vibrations
Thoughts reach others

Just like we are sensitive
To energies they are too

Be tolerant
Be patient

Don't be flustered
If they are negative

Don't work up
Our mind and thoughts

About what they
Are doing, conniving

The stories we cook
Are worse than what is

Overthinking complicates
Thoughts and feelings

Just keep our positivity
Refuse to accept any negativity

No matter what
We are receiving

We must emanate
Peaceful positive vibes

That's the only way
To resolve conflict

Just have complimentary
Thoughts and vibes

Energy is everything
Everything is energy

Keep the energy
And vibrations favourable

Things will sort out
The upheavals will rest

Sooner than we think
When we are positive and happy

Paridhei 🙏 🖤 🤍

38

LEAVE BEHIND

Leave behind

All the thoughts
Emotions, feelings
Anger, hatered
Dislike, discontent
All the problems
Difficulties
And their solutions
Stress, anxiety
Tension, depression

Leave behind

All the questions
And the answers
All the discord
Also all the
Amiability
All the aversions
And dislikes
All the attractions
And desires

Leave behind

All the work
That needs to
Be done, that
Seems unavoidable
All that has to
Be achieved
All the gains
All the losses

Leave behind

All in the
Material world
Which seems
Important today
All that seems
Unignorable
All that is
Screaming for
Our attention

Leave it all behind

Just sit for
Sometime
In awareness
In meditation
Focussing on
Nothing external
Just you and
Your awareness

Connect to
The universe
The supreme being
The greater force

Let the higher
Energy flow
Through you
Realise the
Superior power

Let it energise you
Let it heal you
Let it pull you up
Let it elate you
Let it bring peace
Let it uplift you

Let your aura expand
Let divine energy
Purify you
Cleanse you
Let you be
A being of light

Meditate regularly

Allow it to bring
Betterment internally
Better inner growth
Better soul evolution

Allow it to bring
Also material success
Better focus
Better peace
Better harmony
Better understanding
Better decision making
Better critical thinking
Sharper mind
Reduced stress anxiety

It gifts us with
Much more success
Much more triumph
Than we can imagine
That is possible
Through just
Hard labour
And physical work

To soar higher
In your inner world
And consequently
In the outer world
Meditate regularly

Lift yourself up
Be at the vanguard
Meditate regularly

Paridhei 🙏 ♡

39

LEAVE THE MOVIE BEHIND

Just as we
Leave
The movie hall
When we step out
We leave
The reel life
Behind

Let's also
Sometimes
Leave
The drama of
Real life
Behind

Just leave it
Just ignore it

Align to a higher energy
Align to the upper levels
Align to the divine

Solutions won't come
By overthinking
Being too submerged
In life

They come
When we're objective
When we're detached

No matter how
Important it is
No matter how
Involved
We are in the
Present moment

Every now and then
Just let go
Just drop it
Just leave it
Just ignore it

And align with
The higher power

Notice how
Unimportant
Life situations are
How futile
The happenings are
How insignificant
Things we give
Importance are

Now when we're
Detached
It'll be easier
To live life
With grace
To solve problems
With ease

Everything falls in place

It will be
Blissful

Every now and then
Leave
The movie of life
Behind

Paridhei 🙏 🖤

40

LET'S KEEP OUR INNER HAPPINESS

Never ever let
The pleasantness
Of our mind
Be affected by
What's happening around us

Let's keep our
Inner happiness
Inner peace, intact
No matter what's
Unfolding outside

It will difficult
It will be tough
To maintain
Evenness amidst chaos
In the turmoil

But when we're
Solving problems
Finding solutions
We will need to be
Happy and peaceful

Otherwise our mind
Will be clogged
We will not find

The path
We will be misled

We will have the haze
Of melancholy
Of upsetness
Of anger or hatred
Not allowing
To see the way ahead

Anxious and flustered
State of mind
Will not bring positive
Results and conclusions
Will give wrong outcome

Keep happy
Keep cheerful
Keep in a good mood
That will have
Positive affect

On the situation
On the people
On the problem
And the solution
Will gradually emerge

Keep happy
Keep cheerful
Keep peaceful
Keep jolly
No matter what

Paridhei 🙏 🖤

41

LET'S WISH OTHER PEOPLE WELL

Let's wish
Other people well
If for nothing else
For our own good

It's so easy
To get angry
Curse, wish hell
To someone who
Hurts us wrongs us

But don't forget
What it will
Do to us

Like even a drop
Of colour
Dropped into water
Mixes spreads
And colours
The entire water

A pinch of
Negativity
Can spread
And colour

Our mind and
Inner self
Our entire heart
And soul

A little bit
Of negativity
Developed
In ourselves
Spreads all over
Affects every
Part of our
Mind body
Heart and soul

Negativity has
Repercussions

Stop that negativity
Nip it
At the bud

Feel hurt
Get over it
Feel angry
Get over it
Feel revenge
Get over it

Ignore the negativity

Act if we must
React if we must
Sort it out
If we must

But don't nurture
Don't hold on
To the negativity

And also still keep
Wishing everyone well
As what
We wish, intend
Bless and spread
Around us
Comes back to us
Multiplied
Many many times

Paridhei

42

LOOK

Look look look
How fast we get affected

How swiftly
Our mood changes

How soon
We become negative

Did you notice ?
Are you aware ?

That's the first step
Most important to be aware

So,
Then,

How to stick to positivity ?
How to be unmoved ?

How to be unshaken ?
How to be undisturbed ?

By the negativity
Building inside us

Just stop
Just do gratitude

Switch your thought to
All things positive around

Be grateful
For what you have

Be grateful
For all the lovely people

Just look for
What you love, you like

Now get back
To whatever you were doing

This will help us
Be firm, be unstirred

Be positive
Be happy

Paridhei

43

LOOK WHERE WE HAVE REACHED

Look where
We have reached

Look how far
We have come

From the days of
Not knowing anything

From the times
We had no control

Grateful for the
Gift of meditation

Humbled by the
Deed of self awareness

Churned by the
Act of self improvement

We stand today
Looking at ourself
From far

These thoughts
These feelings
Not always affecting us

As if there's an
Invisible screen

From which
We can keep
All negativity at bay

We can look at it
From far
Unaffected by it

Such a blessing
Such a boon
Awareness
Objectivity
Detachment

Super thankful
To my gurus
Master choa &
Guru padmasambhava

Paridhei

44

LOVE YOURSELF
DO GOOD WORK

Couldn't ever
Stress more
On self-love
On self-respect
On self-worth

You will only get
In life
What you think
You're worthy of

Find yourself
Worthy of love
Love yourself
You'll get love

Find yourself
Worthy of respect
Respect yourself
You'll get respect

Find yourself
Worthy of worth
Recognise your own
Worth

You'll get people
Who recognise
Your worth

Life is too short
Life is too valuable

You have a lot to do
You have a lot to
Work for
A lot of it on yourself

So much difference
To make
So much to
Contribute
So much to
Serve more
Do more
Be more

To make yourself
Better and better
To make this world
A better place

Just go find your tribe
Find people
Of mutual
Respect
Love
Care
Affection
Worth
Cooperation

Find people
You gel with
Make your team
And go do your job

You never know
There will be some
Who are also
Looking for someone
Like you
Who also
Have similar
Visions missions

Don't waste time
On someplace
That's not happening
Connect
Collaborate
Collect your tribe

Don't worry about
Who loves you
Not
Who reciprocates
Not
Not worth
Deliberating on
Those few
It's ok
Move on

You love yourself

Don't keep
Thinking
Why how
Why not
How come

Focus on
Inside of you
And outside
Of you
Focus on
What work
You want to do
On yourself
And the world
What difference
You want to make
To yourself
To your surroundings
To the world

Only when you
Love yourself
You can love
Anyone else

Love yourself
Go ahead
Find your tribe
People who love you
Love them back

Get together
Concentrate
Do significant
Good work

Make yourself
Brilliant
Make this world
A better place

Paridhei 🙏 ♥

45

MANIFESTATION

So we
Know the power of
Our thoughts

We know
What we
Think strongly
Desire dearly
Manifests

So what of it?

What do we
Want to truly
Manifest ?

Do we know
What we truly want ?
What we should do ?
What we must have ?
What we should aim for ?
What will make us happy?

Many a times
We don't

Sometimes we feel,
Like, desire, something
But get distracted
Or even discouraged

Sometimes we aim
For something
And get it
And then feel
That's not what
We wanted
And we're not
Completely happy

Confusing isn't it?

To be truly happy,
Happy by our
Manifestation
We must know
What is our true
Divine purpose

What's the point
Of manifesting
And feeling empty
And wanting
More and more

Align to the
Divine purpose
To truly know
Why we are here

Aim high
Live our
True purpose
True potential

Only that
Will give us
True happiness

Otherwise
We can keep
Manifesting
But we'll still
Be searching and
Searching
And forever
Be dissatisfied

Paridhei 🙏 🖤

46

MASTERING ONESELF

Mastering oneself
Is the intelligent thing to do

It's the prerequisite
For success

It's the first thing
We ought to deal with

Nothing is
More challenging

But nothing more
Satisfying too

Nothing more important
Nothing more essential

No matter what
We want to do

We will use ourself only
Better to sharpen ourself

The one tool we have
The one instrument we have

We have to handle the world
With ourselves only

Better to work on ourselves
To get better output

To achieve anything and win
We will need our best

Whatever we aim for
Wish to achieve

We will face maximum
Hinderance from the self

Better to
Perfect ourselves

To get the
Best performance

We need happiness
We need perfect peace

Only working on ourselves
Will bring lasting happiness

Paridhei 🙏 ♥

47

MAY MY WILL MATCH

God almighty and my guru
May my will
Match yours

May i want
What you want
For me

May there be
No conflict
Between

What you think
Is good for me
And what i want

If there is
Then may your
Will prevail

And may i never
Be disheartened
By what you give me

May i never
Be disappointed
From what i receive

May i never
Be discouraged
From good work

By the results
Of what i try to do
What comes to me

May i try my best
Aim high and big
May that be aligned

To your wishes
To your desires
To your blessings

And if it's different
Then let it be
Your choice

And there be
No doubt
In my mind

That you will give me
The most appropriate
The best for me

For me and my well being
I gracefully
With full trust and faith

Accept what you
Have planned for me
What you bless me with

Paridhei 🙏 🖤

48

MAY PEACE BE WITH US

May peace be with us
Peace within
Peace outside
Peace in our thoughts
Peace in our actions

Peace in our breath
Every inhale brings
In peace
Every exhale takes
Out chaos

No disturbances
No internal mayhem
No external confusion
No doubt of it
No cynicism on peace

Just peace peace peace
Our entire aura
Full of peace
Emanating peace
Causing peace around

The misunderstandings
The wrong judgements
The bewilderment

That caused disturbance
All cleared, all sorted

Crystal clear thoughts
A pellucid path seen
All the waves subside
Correct actions prompted
Peaceful measures opted

This is the effect of
Meditation and techniques
The solutions reveal
The perplexity clear
I thank the guru for these gifts

The techniques taught
To us in our school
The meditations given to us
Help us to the path of peace
To solving life puzzles

What seems disarray
What seems a mystery
What seems difficult
At times even impossible
Becomes easy and tranquil

By the gift of meditation
And the amazing techniques
Thank you to our guru
Thank you to our seniors
Thank you to our school

The pranic healing school

49

MEDITATE

With the background
Of ignorance
How will we get ahead
How will we reach higher

When we don't have
A support
Of inner growth
How will we go far

When our resolve
Itself is incorrect
How will we
Achieve anything

When our perspective
Is skewed
How will we find out
The solutions to problems

Our guru taught us to

Meditate meditate meditate
To make right resolutions
To make correct decisions
To have the fair point of view

And not only meditate
Purify ourselves
Do good deeds
Build our karmic account

These are the things

Which will take us far
We will help us touch
Higher heights
Achieve more materially and spiritually

Work on ourselves
Remove all negatives
Improve ourselves
And meditate regularly

That will get us
True success!

Paridhei 🙏 ♥

50

MEDITATE

If you really
Want to liberate
Your mind
Meditate

If you want to
Set yourself
Free
Meditate

It's unbelievable
How our mind
Is stuck up
With so many things

How it's entangled
In the web of life
In the jumble of
Unnecessary thoughts
Useless noise and clutter

Sometimes we
Know this
Sometimes we don't
Even know

Sometimes we
Realise
We're in
The labyrinth
We're lost
Sometimes we
Don't

There's so much
Power in us
We don't see
There's so much
Potential in us
We don't know

We truly want
To see ourselves
Know ourselves
Live our potential
Be free

Then let's meditate
Meditate
Meditate

Paridhei 🙏 🖤

51

MY LIMITATIONS

When surrounded
By difficulties
I realised my limitations
Stood out more than
Any other factor

As the real
Reasons for
Hinderances
And blocks
And delays and failures

They were really
Limiting my ability
To handle the problem
Get out of
The tricky situation

So realised the need
For self-improvement
Self-mastery
And self-purification
Continuous self-introspection

Only through these
Could i ever
Defeat the enemy
Mostly inside me
Some outside me too

The tough situations
Seemed easy
When i mastered
Myself and
Removed follies

Thanking almighty
And the guru
For throwing light
On the dark allies
Inside me

Lighting the path
Showing the way
To self-perfection
And mastering
The art of life

Paridhei 🙏 🖤

52

MY PRAYERS
MY BLESSINGS TODAY

May mother earth
Be rejuvenated
Be revitalised
May all the plants
Animals thrive
May all humans
Have harmonious
Peaceful happy lives

May the lovely birds
Flying around
Gliding here and there
Hopping from one
Tree to another
Chirping around
Be blessed
May they have
A wonderful life

May all the beautiful
Trees all around us
Intricate network
Of branches
Different shapes
Sizes of leaves

Variety of green shades
Giving us cover
Be fresh and alive
Now and forever

May the crispy clear
Morning
The magnanimous
Sunlight
Bright cheerful day
The soft breeze
Blowing and spreading
Good vibes
Continue to bring
Happiness and cheer in
Everyone's lives

May all the wild animals
Birds,fish, aquatic animals
Living everywhere
Open in the jungles
And in zoos and parks
Thrive and flourish
The smallest of the
Smallest living being
On this planet earth
Be blessed and beatified

May everyone reading
This poem
Be blessed with
Divine light divine love
Divine power
Divine protection
Divine guidance
Divine help and mercy

May you have a bright
Sparkling sunshine
Life full of
Happiness peace
Abundance at all levels

May my prayers be
Answered
May my blessings
Be materialised
May all such
Well meaning desires
Of every person
Every being
Attain fulfilment

A prayer inspired by
The atmosphere around me
The beautiful view,
The lovely weather,
The birds and animals
Around me

Paridhei

53

NEGATIVE THOUGHTS

Those negative
Thoughts
And feelings
That we generate
Due to some
Or the other
Cause or effect

They will affect
Us only
They will bring
Us down only

They will cause
Harm to us only
Physically mentally

They will affect
Our health
Our well being

So is it worth it ?
Whatever be the
Reason
Or the trigger

So is it worth it ?
Whoever we
Blame
Whoever we
Put the onus on

We have to realise
That negativity
It's in us only
Inside us only
We are incharge
We are to blame
We are responsible

We are the cause
We are the effect
We are the problem

Why suffer when
We can change it
Change the thought
Switch the thought
Keep happy
Keep positive

Steer clear of
That negativity
That resentment
That frustration
That jealousy
That anger
That hatered

We can do it
It's in our hands
Let's keep happy
Let's keep positive

Paridhei 🙏 🖤

54

NEGATIVITY

The negativity we build on the
The negative that happens

Is much more than
What actually happens

Someone did something
Somethings happen

Something said, something seen
Affects alright

But we don't need to
Build up more story on it

Let's not make
A mountain out of a mole hill

Let's not spin a web of negativity
Of thoughts feelings emotions

On just something small
That occurs or we notice

Felt something negative
Feel it, accept it, ignore it

Don't think too much on it
Don't add spice to it

Do not react
Just think and act

It will surely be much less
Than what we perceive

Be happy 🖤
Keep smiling 🖤

Paridhei 🙏🖤

55

NO LIFE LIKE A LIFE BEING AN INSTRUMENT OF THE GURU

No life like a life being an
Instrument of the guru

The best way
Is the guru's way
The best path
Is the path shown
By the guru

Best work
Is the work
Of the guru
No doubts
No stress

Best way to live
Is to be
An instrument
Of the guru
Just give our best

Living in the
Guru's shadow
Living in his aura

Can get us places
Can take us high

Somewhere
We couldn't
Go on our own
Couldn't achieve
On our own

Life becomes easy
When we have
The wisdom
Of the guru
Guiding us

Life has more
Meaning when
We can do service
Under the supervision
Of the guru

Life has value
When we live
The guru's dream
And have his
Noble mission

Living with the
Guru is precious
It's the most
Valuable gift
That we can ever get

Deep deep gratitude
And big thank you
To guru master choa

And mahaguruji meiling
For always keeping
Me with them

Remembering master choa
The founder of modern pranic healing and arhatic yoga
On his mahasamadhi day. 🙏🖤

Paridhei 🙏🖤

56

NOTHING IS BEYOND OURSELVES

All the problems
We have
All the difficulties
All the challenges
All the tough times

Can simply be
Boiled down to
One reason
Our very own selves
Our own mind

Nothing is more
And beyond
Our own selves
We ourselves
Are the cause

Of every suffering
Of every pain
Of every agony
That we went through
That we go through now

No point blaming
Other people, relationships
Circumstances, situations
Events, occurrences
Or the state of affairs

Nothing could have
Caused the inferior situation
Other than us, our mind,
Our thoughts, our feelings
Our demeanour, our attitude

It's time we take
The responsibility
Own up to our own
Misgivings and follies
The sooner the better

It's the wise thing to do
Realise we're at fault
Try to make amends
Improve ourselves
Work on ourselves

When we change
Ourselves
We will change
The circumstance
We will make it better

If anyone is responsible
It's we ourselves
Only change to make
Is in ourselves
We are the specimen to work on

To make the situation
Beautiful, pleasant
Loving, favourable,
Change ourselves
Make ourselves better

Paridhei 🙏 ♥

57

ONLY ALL ABOUT US

There'll be days
When everything
May just not fit

Days when there
Will be turmoil
Be total chaos

Those days
We have
To remember

It's not about
The situation
The external state

The people around
That person who
Hurt us

Not that consequence
Which is unearthed
Not the circumstances

It's only all about us
The tension building
Inside, is all ours

The upheavals
We feel
Are all our own doing

We will know this
We will be aware
We will try to steer clear

We may distance
Ourselves from
This turbulence

Sometimes
Remove all disorder
On our own

Sometimes
Just be able
To clear the mess

But still there will
Be times,
Occasions

When we will
Succumb,
Give in

Give in to the
Pressure
Dissolve in the

Negativity,
Situations,
State of affairs

We may
Even become
One with it

It has happened
To me
So many times

Just those days
When we can't
Solve the problems

Find our way
Absolve all negativity
Find peace

We try everything
We know
And it doesn't work

Those days are
The days when
My gurus teachings

Have helped me
The use of energy
Has helped me

Pranic healing
The techniques
And the tools

Have helped me
Surface
From under the muck

Believe me
They are miraculous
They are amazing

Have helped many
Others also,
With the technology

When we have
Such easy and
Effective and efficient

Help available
Why worry
Why just not try it

Do try it out
You'll get better
Within no time

Things will
Become positive
In a jiffy

We will change
The world around us
Will change

We will find
Mental peace and
Happiness unbound

Do try it
Try pranic healing
And make life work

For you
For everyone
Around you

Paridhei 🙏 🖤

58

ONLY WHEN WE …..

Only when we think of other people
Their problems
Their difficulties

Will we be free of ourselves
Our problems
Our difficulties

Only when we are
Empathetic towards others
Feel for their misery

Will our perils
Fly away
Our troubles
Just dissolve

Only when we offer help
Are compassionate to others
In their time of need
In their tough situations

Will we get help
In our own chaos
In our jeopardy
In this complicated life

Only when we share
And care with others
Will we receive abundance
In our life

To get love help health wealth abundance and prosperity
We will need to give, bless others
With the same

What we give
Only that will come to us
In the measure we give
Only that will come to us

Paridhei 🙏 🖤

59

OUR INNER SELF

Nothing
On the outside
Will work
If we have not
Dealt with
Our inner self
First

No matter
What act
We put up
How we behave

If we haven't
Sorted our
Inner self
It will surely
Surface
Glimpses will be
Shown
And they will
Reveal our
Internal follies

Even if our
Outer self
Is not upto
The mark
But the inner self
Is worthy
We can get away

But if our
Outer self is
Polished
And our inner self
Is dark
We can never
Get away

So
Work work work
Work on
Ourselves
That's what we
Ought to do

Get our inner self
Right
And we will see
Ourselves
Blossoming
Succeeding
Everywhere

And meditation helps
Construct a better
Inner self

Paridhei 🙏 🖤

60

OUR SECRET DESIRE: PERFECTION

We all want perfection
We secretly crave it

We want our relationships
To be perfect
We want our work
To be perfect
We want our health
To be perfect
We want our bodies to
To be perfect
We want our surroundings
To be perfect
We want our home
To be perfect
We want our world
To be perfect
We want everything
To be perfect

We all secretly
Desire perfection

And when we don't get it
We're upset, sad, angry

But perfection is
An illusion

What's the definition
Of perfection?

Is it not different
For everyone ?

Does it not vary
For us ourselves?

Perfection changes
Meaning with situations

The only perfection
Possible and
Should be desired

Is the taming of our mind
Is the control of our thoughts
And feelings and emotions

When that is achieved
Everything in us and around us
Will be perfect

We will live in a dream world
Where imperfections exist
But they won't affect us

Total freedom
Total happiness
No suffering

Paridhei 🙏 ♡

61

OUR TRUE INNER SELF

I have realised

That we constantly look for
Something new
Something beautiful
Something special

But when we get that
After a while
When it's no longer
A novelty

We no longer
Are stimulated by it
No longer entertained by it
No longer find it special

The newness
The uniqueness
The interest
Fades away too soon

What's the answer ?
What's the solution?

Be at peace
With yourself now
Just this moment
Be happy
Wherever you're at

Let your true
Inner nature inner self
Be at peace and happy
No matter what

Pursue your dreams
Go after your ambitions
Let the drive be there
Keep the fire alive

But be content
Peaceful happy
Right now
In the present too

Don't let the moment
Be governed by
Anything else
Than this true nature

Paridhei 🙏 🖤

62

PEACE

I've noticed
One thing
Once our peace
Gets disturbed

It could be due
To any trigger
Or could be
In any area

If our tranquility
Gets ripples
It affects everything
All other areas too

Those ripples
Spread all across
They don't limit
To the trigger

Like the waves
In placid waters
When we throw
A stone

They spread far
And wide
The ripples
Form waves

They take their
Own time
To subside
To calm down

We can put
Our hand in
The water
Or something else

To try to
Stop those ripples
They don't
Get in control

Just like that
Our mind
Once disturbed
Takes time

How fast
It will fall back
Into peace
Depends

Depends on
How we have
Conditioned it
Trained it

Awareness
That there has
Been disturbance
Is the first step

Knowing the trigger
Helps
And dealing with it
There only

Acceptance
That there's
Perturbation
Will also help

How fast
We come back
To normal thereafter
We need to see

How to train?
Meditation helps
Concentration
On breath helps

Through continued
Practice and training
We can reduce
This time to get back

Slowly slowly
We have to move
To when
Our peace remains

Forever
Nothing affects it
We are in our
Peaceful self always

We continue to
Our daily tasks
And life, detached
Do our actions

But, no disturbance
No disruption
Just the peace
This is ideal

But we can do it!

Paridhei 🙏 🖤

PEACE INSIDE

No matter
What's happening
Around us
Let's
Keep our inside
At peace

Understand
That whatever is
Going on
It doesn't have
To disturb our inside

Nothing should
Shake us
Perturb us
Imbalance us
From inside

Handle the outside
On the outside
Don't let anything
Affect our inside

Act react
Perform
Outside
From an
Inner source of
Inner peace

It may be difficult
But it's not impossible

That's why
We should meditate
So that we have
Awareness
And control

That's why
We need to pray
That we achieve
This perfection

All's possible when
The source
Is the
The divine

Paridhei 🙏🖤

64

PERCEPTIONS

Remember that
Our judgement
Our decisions
Our actions
Are based on
Our perceptions

And our perceptions
Are greatly flawed
As they depend
On our wisdom

And our wisdom
Is not upto
The mark

No matter
How much
We know
How much
Intelligence
We have

We will still
Fall short
We will never

Know
All sides all angles
Of things

Our mind
Our thoughts
Are foggy
With our
Own follies
Own prejudices

As there are
Infinite
Solutions
Innumerable
Permutations
Combinations

So let's always
Pray for
Divine guidance
Divine wisdom
Divine intervention
Divine knowledge

So that we are
Guided helped
To the right
Understanding
Right knowledge
Right actions

Paridhei

65

PERFECT OURSELVES

Sometime down the line
When i was aiming high
Being ambitious
I realised i needed
To build myself stronger
Internally mentally
Grow and evolve inside

To gain materially
Be successful
Get wealth
Prosperity, abundance
Even just for
The small wins i want,
To fulfill my dreams

I need to concentrate
On inner growth
That no matter
What i do externally
It won't matter
Till it's backed up
By development inside

But while working
On myself
Building myself from
Inside
I realised that
That's all that
Is to life

Inner growth
Inner evolution
The learning
The process
Of improving
Of growing internally
Is all that matters

All the external
Achievements
Dwarfed and became
Less important
What got left behind
Was just a thirst
For inner growth

Not for anything else
But just to
Evolve the soul
To purify myself
To become better
And better
To progress inside

It's an addiction
To inner growth
To improving myself
To excel in

The art of self-
Development
To prefect myself

What we take
With us is just
All of this
Nothing external
No material gain
Will go with us
This is true wealth

True abundance
True achievement
Something which
No one can take away
Not even death
And it grows
Exponentially

Life of course
Becomes easy
We attract
All material gain
All the opulence
Effortlessly and abundantly
When we build ourselves

But it's a never
Ending process
And soon we build
Ourselves
Just for better growth
Nothing else

Just to prefect
Ourselves
Become a better
Version of ourselves
That becomes our
Ambition
Our purpose for life

Paridhei 🙏 🖤

66

PERSISTENCE

Dear surya and durga

Our success in anything
Will finally boil down
To persistence

Because even desire
Will fluctuate

Whenever we encounter
Obstacles and difficulties
We may not want
To do the work anymore

We should not give up
Not giving up
Or giving up
Will become a habit

It's not limited to
One field or task
It could be anything we do
Sports
Studies
Business
Profession

Art
Performing arts
Hobbies
Across the gamut
Only persistence
Will get us there

We will have
The problems
Face tough
Situations
Adversities
Go through
Difficult times
Ups and downs
In all of these
And every field
Of our life

Also
Believing in ourselves
Helps
Having positive thoughts
Helps

We should never ever
Leave our belief
In ourselves
That we can do it

We should never allow
Negative thoughts
To enter our system

We truly will have to
Watch our belief
And our thoughts
These are powerful tools
That could work for us
Or against us too

Armed with trust
And belief in ourselves
And positive thoughts
We will be able to persist

And with persistence
We will make it there

Paridhei 🙏 🖤

67

POSITIVE THOUGHTS

Nothing can substitute
Positive thinking
Not all the intelligence we have
Not all the talent we have
Not all the wealth we have
Not all the contacts we have
Not all the work we put in
Not all the strength we have
Not all the good health we have
Not all the carefulness with
Which we tread

If we do not have
Positive thinking
Everything will crumble
Nothing will be achieved
No success guaranteed

But if we have
Positive thinking
And we don't have
Anything else
At the moment

It's only a matter of time
We will soon
Have everything !

Paridhei 🙏 🤍

68

PRAY FOR WISDOM

Wisdom wisdom wisdom
That's what we should pray for

If we have more and more wisdom
Our lives would be so much easier

Wisdom to differentiate
The good from the bad

Wisdom to know in any impulse
What's right, what's wrong

Wisdom to think and analyse fast
And decide the best action

Wisdom to decipher the right path
In the middle of even chaos

Wisdom to know how to behave, act
In the most challenging circumstances

Wisdom to know what to do
In the midst of confusing situations

Wisdom so we make less mistakes
And always do the correct action

Wisdom to be peaceful and content
Though we may aspire for more

Wisdom to choose happiness
No matter what's happening around

As wisdom leads to happiness
And happiness leads to wisdom

Wisdom to choose and yearn
For more wisdom over anything else

Because no matter we have and acquire
Will be a waste if we don't have wisdom

Paridhei 🙏 🖤

69

PROBLEMS

There'll be problems
Everywhere, no matter
What we choose to do
 Or where we are at

If one situation
Has x problems
Another situation
Will have y problems

Even when
We're billionaires
We'll have some or
The other tight spots

Even if we're the pm
We'll have many
And more
Tough situations

So achieving,
Reaching somewhere
Is no guarantee
Of not having difficulties

The only thing
That will help is
Keeping neutral
Keeping positive

We need to learn
To keep our peace
No matter what
No matter where

We should
Deal with problems
Objectively
Not to affect us

It's in our thoughts
It's in our minds
That most problems exist
That's where they dwell

Checking our
Mind and thoughts
Keeping them positive
Will solve most of them

So it's not
A problem free world
We need to dream of
We need to wish for

But pray for the tact
The ability, the skill
To face and tackle
Any kind of situation

Whatever that
May present itself
In our lives
In our worlds

Paridhei 🙏♥

70

SEEK THE DIVINE

In this life surrounded by
Myriad of illusions

We will need guidance
We will need help

To know which path to take
Between the web of pathways

So many ways
Each taking us to different realities

Each decision leading us
To a different world

Every step transporting
Us to a different scenery

Better to seek divine help
To grant us wisdom

For the correct step
For the right choice

What to do
In every situation, in every scenario

What we choose
Will lead us to a new world

Let's pray for the best decision
Let's pray for what is right for us

No matter how hard we try
Without divine help would be lost

Our wisdom is limited
Our understanding stunted

Better to take the help
Of the supreme being

That's why it's important
To sit and pray and meditate

On the higher self
On the guru, the higher beings

To show us the way
To show us the path

To bring light
To this darkness of ignorance

So that we live a life
Best for us, ideal for us

Away from anything wrong
So that we are karmically entitled

To shine with love and light
Happy diwali 🪔

Paridhei 🙏🤎

71

SELF-DISCOVERY

The beauty of
Self-discovery
I wouldn't exchange
For anything

Exploring myself
Knowing myself
What makes me tick
Who am i

What are truly
My positives
What are the
Follies i have within

What are the
Mistakes i am
Making and can make
My hidden errors

What is the strength
Inside me
What is the
Latent potential

Awakening to
My inner self
Control of
Myself buried in me

The mysterious self
That goes unnoticed
By me myself
That's not clear from top

What all i will give
For this knowledge
For this precious
Inner quest

No pursuit
Like the pursuit
Of the self
Of the inner me

No such glamour
Not much attraction
To something else
It's just me

When we know
Ourselves
Can control
Ourselves

We can control
The world
The key to the
Universe is the self

Better to plunge
Into this discovery
Only then
Look for anything out

Paridhei 🙏 ♥ 🦋

72

STAND TALL

Stand tall and peaceful
Amidst the chaos of life

Watch the facade
The illusions

Which life throws
At you

Be undisturbed
Be undeterred

From your
Peaceful countenance

Everything that
Sways will calm down

Anything that's
Boiling will cool down

All the mayhem
The confusion

Will get sorted
In some time

Faster if we
Maintain calm

There are too many
Variables

Myriad of options
To choose from

Easier to choose
When we are tranquil

Being harmonious
Being cheerful

At this point
Extremely pertinent

Maintain a
Pacific demeanour

To flow smoothly
Through the rapids of life

Paridhei 🙏 ♡

73

STOP

Stop

Take a few steps back
Mentally just zoom out

For a few moments
Just be an observer

Don't be the engrossed
Doer

Just be the detached
Observer

Notice what's happening
Without being attached

Watch your thoughts
Watch your mind

Watch the happenings
Watch the surroundings

Watch your actions
Watch your reactions

You'll get a better
Perspective

When you observe
Detached

Now take cognisance
Of your thoughts

Now take a objective view
Of the situation

Now decide
What to do

Isn't it easier now

It's easier to take
The right decision

When we are not
Emotionally entangled

When we are detached
Have the complete view

We will not go wrong
In our actions

Paridhei 🙏 🖤 🤍

74

THAT ONE THOUGHT

Look back
And see

That one thought
Made all
The difference

The repetition
And sustenance
Of
That one thought
Made all the difference

Could have been
A positive one
Or
A negative one

But it paved
The way for
A different direction
A different outcome

Different from
Some other
Outcome that
Might have been
Maybe different than
What we might
Have wanted

So it's just
A matter of
Dealing with
That one thought
Catching
That one thought
Changing
That one thought
If required

Only awareness of
That one thought
Only controlling
That one thought

Actually
The rest we
Build on
That one thought
We act on the
Story we build on
That one thought

To be aware
To be cautious
To control it

To keep
That one thought
Positive

Because at
One time
There is just
That one thought
In our mind

We need awareness
We need to know
Which one is
Positive
And which one is
Negative
Which one is
Getting us down
Which one is
The best for
Positive results

All this is
Possible
Through meditation

Through which
We will have
Awareness
Knowledge
And control
Over
That one thought

We should think
Only that
Which lifts us
And our life up
And keeps
Us and it positive

Paridhei 🙏 ♡

THE PITFALLS OF THE NEGATIVE

When i see people
Who harness the evil
Nurture the bad
Thinking that it's good

Musing only about
The short term gain
Only looking
At the profit at hand

Sometimes i do feel
Maybe i should also
Use the negative
And win big time

Be the winner
Of the present moment
Make large gains
Be one up on the rivals

But then wisdom prevails
And i know, as is taught
That it's better to stick
With the positive

Let me not have
A constricted view
Of the path
Of life as a whole

The pitfalls of negative
Far outweigh
The gains that we earn
For the short time

The downfall that comes
With sticking to the dark
Is phenomenal
And it takes lots of time

To recover
To get back on track
To gain the path
To be back to positive

The profits of the positive
And pure and virtuous
Are long term
And stay with us lifetimes

I wouldn't want to
Ever trade my
Inner growth
The spiritual path

For something
As mundane as
The worldy gain
Which looks huge today

But it will be dwarfed
In front of
Innermost growth
Spiritual evolution

May i never go
Towards the negative
May i stay forever
Pure pure pure

May i soar
Higher and higher
In the inner plane
In the supreme world

So be it

Paridhei 🙏 🩷

76

THE QUEST FOR HAPPINESS

The quest is for happiness
Everlasting happiness, isn't it ?

Aren't we all after it ?
Searching and exploring

We use many ways
To satisfy our, this urge

Entertainment, amassing wealth
Buying things, dress up, socialising,

Building social network, partying
Playing sports, watching tv,

Films, clubs, bars, pubs
Concerts, etc, we try it all

We wander, we roam
We keep thirsting for it

But the more we indulge, we realise
The elation ends too soon

It's short lived
It doesn't last long

We keep looking
For happiness on the outside

When all we need to do is,
Is plunge inside

Deep internal focus, concentration on the inner self,
higher energies

Perfecting oneself
Freedom from weaknesses, faults

Devotion to the higher beings
Supreme almighty, divine forces

Service, kindness,
Loving others, all beings,

Helping others, acts of mercy
Healing others, praying for others

These are the things which bring
Everlasting happiness

I know
Because i've tried it

If not convinced
Try it yourself

Don't pursue happiness outside
Look for it inside yourself

Perfecting the art of higher life
Will bring everlasting true happiness

Paridhei 🙏 🖤

77

THE SECRET IS ....

Haven't we heard about
Those sages who sat,
Still sit, in meditation
For years together

The enlightened ones
Who could go
For days together
Without food, water, sleep

Don't think
They ate or drank much
They slept little
And just kept on

So many of them
Lived on alms
On donations
On generosity of others

Doing nothing particular
Themselves
No livelihood
Just living a spiritual life

How do they survive?
Without proper diet
Proper occupation
Proper income

How do some of them,
Also live hectic lives
Work all day
Meet people all day

They pack into
Their lives in 24 hrs
So much more than
What we can ever do

What is it that they do
How do they manage it
Where do they get
The extra energy from

Their secret is
Divine energy
They survive on
Spiritual energy

They generate
So much of positivity
So much of godly energy
In their aura chakras

Their aura, chakras
Are free from
All negativity
All chaos

Dark forces
Don't touch them
Their systems
Are pure and bright

Thoughts positive
Emotions harmonious
No upheavals
Peace and calm

We too need to
Work better, be healthier
Live our potential
Achieve success

Let's also build
Divine energy
Strengthen our
Etheric body

Let's also pray,
Meditate regularly
Think positive thoughts
Keep negativity at bay

To shine
Wherever we are
To live a
Bright beautiful life

Paridhei 🙏 ♡

78

THINK WHAT YOU WANT

What we are today
Is a reflection of
What we have been thinking,
And doing in the past

We can't be anything
That we haven't imagined
It's in our thoughts
That lies the key of what we are

To manifest differently
We ought to have
Thought differently
Acted differently

So choose wisely
Think and act today
In a manner to get results
Like what you want

Don't think thoughts
That give you results
That you don't want
That are vaguely different

Just think what you want
Align your actions to that
No place for anything else
Manifest the life of your dreams

Paridhei 🙏 🖤

79

THOUGHTS CONTROL

Where are thoughts
Coming from ?

Who has put them there
In our mind ?

They seem to pop up
Out of nowhere
Sometimes
With no context
Sometimes
With no connection

One after the other
Out of ether
They keep flowing

Where are they
Coming from ?

They're coming from
Old conditioning
Repeated emotions
Experiences
Habits

To change them
To make them
Always positive
Always constructive

We need to be
 In control
Control our
Conditioning
Emotions
Experiences
Habits

How do we be
In control?

By being aware
By taking conscious
Efforts to keep
Them in control

Meditation helps
In building awareness
In the conscious efforts
In control

So that we keep
Positive
All the time

So that we become
Thoughtless too
When we want to

Meditate regularly

80

TIME

Time is relative
When we're enjoying
And happy
Time seems to run fast
When we're sad
And unhappy
Time seems to go slow

The same five minutes
Will have
A different duration
In our lives and mind
Depending on
What's the situation
Good or bad

So then how
Will we
Increase the duration
When we're happy
And reduce the duration
When we're sad
How do we have even time

The trick is to
Concentrate on our breath
Control the breath
If our breath is even
In good and bad times
In peaceful and
Traumatic times

Time will even out
Bad times will not
Put us out of breath
Put us out of balance
So also good times
Will not cause
Rustling of our self

It's not easy
But by practicing
Breathing
We can get it
It's taught in yogic texts
And is the true reason
For all spiritual practices

If we can master breath
And have even breath
No matter what's happening
We will master time too
Unaffected we will be
Living peacefully
And happily, always

Walking talking
Eating resting
Working, enjoying
Just concentrate

On our breath
Have even breath and time
That's perfect happiness

That's what we want
Isn't it ?
Eternal happiness
Timeless and boundless

Paridhei 🙏 🖤

81

TO BE HAPPY FOR OTHERS

To be happy for
Other's happiness

To be happy for
Other's success

To be happy for
Other's achievements

To be happy for
Other's abundance

That is the skill
The art, to acquire

If we really want
To be happy ourselves

To be at peace
With ourselves 🏵 🏵

Most of the time
We have everything

Much more than
What we need

But we're just sad
Just melancholy

Comparing and
Competing with others

We surround ourselves
With unhappy thoughts

Thinking of what
Others have and we don't

Totally forgetting our
Own abundance

We get busy
Looking at other's life 🌸 🌸

Imagine the happiness
We will have

When we learn to also
Be happy for others

So many more reasons
We will have to be happy

The love and happiness
Good wishes and prayers

We do for others
Comes back to us

Multiplied many times
In every way

We must learn
To be happy for others

Paridhei 🙏 🖤

82

UNIVERSE INSIDE US

It's amazing
How we humans
Are investing
Time energy effort
In exploring
The universe
Expanding our reach

We say it's vast
It's huge
It's mysterious,
We're curious
We're ambitious
Some also want to
Conquer space

What about
The entire universe
Which is inside us
And immediately
Around us
In our aura
In our chakras

How come we're
Ignorant of it
And we're also
Ignoring it more
Not paying
Any attention to it
Not bothering about it

It has so much
Potential
So much more
Energy and power
Than we give
Credit to
Than we are aware of

If we concentrate
On energising
Rejuvenating
Revitalising
Giving our aura
Chakras and inside us
Enough attention

We will realise
The immense
Power
This universe has
Hidden inside it,
We could cause
A full big bang !

As our guru
Also ancient sages
Have taught us
That when we expand
Our consciousness
When we meditate
When we go beyond

We will unearth
Such capabilities
Such possibilities
We can never imagine
Exist or are possible
Which are beyond
Our comprehension

The human body
The mind and aura
Are capable of doing
Somethings we think
Are impossible,
We may not know of
We may never find out

So, let's dwell into
This unknown
Let's also explore this
This universe
Inside and around us
It's easily available
But we need to work on it

Let's meditate
Let's purify ourselves
So that these capabilities
Are within our reach
And we can do more
Achieve more materially,
Spiritually and serve more

Paridhei 🙏 🖤

83

WANT PEACE?

Human conflict is normal
As we have
Different minds
Different thoughts

Different desires
Different backgrounds
Different grooming
Different reactions

We are different !

It's ok to have a
Different point of view
A discord over
Maybe even futile things

A conflict, a friction
Over anything or everything
We may even verbally
Fight, have heated discussions

But violence? Brutality ?
Savagery ? War?
Is that required ?
Is it possible to stop it ?

We forget one thing
We are inter-connected
Everything that we think and do
Affects everyone around us

The emotion, the feelings
The sentiments
That one feels affects
Every other person

Just like a herd of horses
When one runs,
One picks up speed
All the others also tend to run

So, the best gift
We can give to humanity
Is being peaceful ourselves
A calm and tranquil self

We can affect people
Around us
With our positivity
With our own composure

Therefore
To evolve ourselves
Is the greatest duty
Of each one of us

Our aura our energy
Extends all around us
As we evolve
People around us also evolve

As we become
Positive, peaceful
All around us also
Become that

Want peace and evolution
Concentrate first on ourselves
That's our responsibility
That's the fasted way

Paridhei 🙏 ♥

84

WATCH OUT

Watch out for
That single
Negative thought
That pops up
In our mind

Which we think
Is just one thought
Not that harmful
Nothing to
Bother about

We ignore it
We let it be
We let our mind
Dwell on it
Let it occupy

Like just one
Drop of colour
Put in water
Can change
The entire water colour

That one thought
Will alter all
Our other thoughts
Our mood
Our emotions

It will make
All of it negative
Cause us to
Take wrong
Actions and deeds

It has a
Multiplying effect
It will generate
More and more
Negativity

So stop that one
Negative thought
Right there
Just nip it
At the bud

Exchange it
With positive
Change ourselves
Our mood
Our emotions

Keep with the
Favourable thoughts
The ones
That bring peace
And happiness

Because that
One thought
Is critical
It has the power
To change

The whole scenario
The entire picture
It's a game changer
It's of life defining
Importance

To keep all and
Everything
Positive and peaceful
Watch that
One thought

Keep it positive

Paridhei 🙏 🖤

85

WATCH WHAT YOU SEND OUT

What we do to others
Will come back to us
Multiplied many many times

Be careful of the energy
We send too
The thoughts
The psychic vibrations

Negative thoughts
Negative energies
Will bounce back
And come back to us
Multiplied many many times

Everything will boomerang
Not only words or actions
Energy and thoughts too

As taught by my guru

Paridhei

86

WE ALL KNOW ……..

We all know what is right
Isn't it ?

In most situations
Each and every scenario

We instinctively know
What's the right thing to do

Then, what happens?
What goes amiss

Why do we act
In some odd manner

Why do we get
Somethings wrong

Even while we are doing the act
The small voice inside us

Tells us, it's wrong
Tells us to look at the right

Why do we still act negatively
Sometimes, do mistakes

So, it all just comes down to
Self control, self mastery

Listening to our own inner voice
To do the right thing

That impulse to act
That instinct to jump into it

And do something
Even if is it's wrong

Can be managed
Can be restrained

Meditation, breathing exercises
Prayers, chants, yoga, satvic diet

All, will help the act
But most importantly

It is the will to be right
Instinct to tread the correct path

That can be achieved
By these practices

Because having the will to do right
Is half way there itself

We do want to be always right
Tread the veracious path

Because, it's a great price
To pay to do something wrong

The karmic repercussions
Are too many

True wisdom is to be careful
Try and be correct all times

Refrain from unwholesome and evil
And stick to the perfect

We can try to get there
By these practices

Paridhei 🙏 ♥

Thanks to guru master choa and pranic healing and arhatic yoga. We have some powerful meditations and wonderful techniques through which we can help ourselves tread the correct path.

87

WE ARE A SMALL SPECK

We are a small speck
Compared to the
Universe
We are minuscule

But let it not
Make us think
We're unimportant
We don't mean anything

Just like a
Small twig that
Falls into a
Placid lake

Creates ripples
All around it
Makes vibrations
Has an impact

This tiny us
Is also capable
Of spreading
Ripples of positivity

We can emanate
Peace and love
We can affect
Healing and well being

Through our energy
Our aura, our thoughts
Our actions
By our care, kindness

Although tiny
And nanoscopic
Our existence
Matters

We can
Make a difference in
Make this world
A better place

We do matter
We are important
This has to be
Remembered

Let's not mistake
It's not for our ego
But to do good work
Be of great service

Paridhei 🙏 ♥

88

WE ARE PERFECT THE WAY WE ARE

You know the truth ?
We are perfect
As we are
We truly are
Whether we believe
It right now or not

Those imperfections
That are glaring at us
Were all meant to be,
In this imperfect world
They are there to be found
They are to be accepted

Just accept that
They are there
Because that's how
It ought to be
As humans we are
Imperfect and flawed

To let them go,
To become better
We need to
Love ourselves first

Just as we are
Unconditional, agape love

The more we push them
Shun them, hate them
The more they will
Surface and be obtrusive
Just accept them
Just welcome them

And watch
Them dissolve
Slowly gradually fade
And then we can
Choose better
Become better

Only acceptance
Of the imperfections
Unadulterated kindness
To ourselves
Will get us to where
We will be perfect

Will get us above

Paridhei 🙏 🖤

89

WE CAN BE HAPPY ANYWHERE

We humans

We adjust to
Whatever situation
We are put in

We adapt to
Whatever environment
We are exposed to

I see villagers
Adjust to lack of development
And live frugally but cheerful

I see urban people
Reconcile to the traffic jams
And pollution and smog

I see poor persons
Live within their means
And enjoy life there

I see rich people
Live in opulence
And happily bask in luxury

A human child born in
Whatever family
Grows up

Adopting the character
The personality of the clan
And the circumstances

So, truly we can be
Happy where ever
We are put and we live

We should remember this
We adapt and adjust
No matter where we are

This should make us
Realise
We can be happy anywhere

And we should stay happy
No matter what
No matter where

While we strive
For whatever we want
We should first stay happy

Because we can do it !
Our entire race does it !
All the time

We are humans
We can be happy
Anywhere

Let's stay happy
No matter what

Paridhei 🙏 🖤

90

WE DO SO MUCH

We do so much
So much for our entertainment
So much to please our mind
So much to stimulate our being

We do so much
So much to satiate our senses
So much to be happy
So much to feel elated

What is our quest ?
What are we after, after all ?
What ever elusive happiness
Are we after ?

Is happiness
Something on the outside ?
Something to acquire ?
Something to obtain?

When we can feel happy
At this moment
Just sitting here
Just sipping tea

Then what are we
Running after ?
What is the struggle ?
What is the scurry?

Where will true
Happiness comes from ?
How are we going to
Get contented ever ?

Happiness is a state of being
It can be achieved anywhere,
We just need to shift
Our thought to it

We just need to
Convince ourselves
Prepare the mind to
Tune it true happiness

Knowing that we
Can be happy now
In this moment
We choose happiness

No matter what we're doing
No matter where we are at
No matter how difficult
It may be

We will not run after it!
We will end the strife!
We will look inside and
We choose happiness now!

Paridhei 🙏 ♥

91

WE HAVE A CHOICE

The mind keeps wandering
Thoughts keep flowing

Every time a thought
Is in the mind
We give it importance
It stays

When we shift to
Another thought
The previous one
Is no longer important

So in all
All thoughts are
Only as important
As we give
Significance to

Meaning
We have a choice
We are in control

Let's put our mind
Where we want it to
Not where it
Wants to wander

Let's take charge
Let's give importance
Only to the positive
Only to the good
Only to the pure

Or even the perfect
No thought at all

Let's gaurd our thoughts
Like treasure

Because thoughts
Will
Affect our actions
Which will
Affect our destiny

Paridhei

92

WE HAVE ALL THE POWER

We are all powerful
We have all the power
We have the energy

We have the power
To change this world

To make it a better place

Never underrate
The power, the influence
The potential we have in us

Never think we are powerless
Coz we have our energy
We have our vibes

We can emanate positivity
We can send positive vibes
We can send complimentary energy

Whatever is going wrong
In the world
We can bless

We can reconstruct
A peaceful world in our mind
And send out positive thoughts

Our energy matters
Our thoughts have the strength
We can transmute the world

Have faith in
Our energy, our thoughts
And pour positivity

It will alter the world
Make it more peaceful
Our blessings will heal people

Never ever underestimate
This power we have in us
This strength this potential in us

It's not only what we can do,
Our thoughts are powerful too
The energy, the blessings all powerful

Never worry if we can't do enough
Do what you can and
Keep sending out positive vibes

A pranic healer's point of view

Paridhei 🙏 🖤

93

WE HAVE TO BE CONVINCED

Peace and happiness
Harmony and tranquility
Are easy to achieve
Are just a step away

The only thing is
We have
To be convinced
We want them

That's the most
Important hurdle
We have to cross,
The first step

Whenever negative
Thoughts and feelings
Upheavals of emotions
Cause turmoil and chaos

At that moment
We have to be ready
Ready to release them
To let them go

That's when we need
To decide and pledge
We don't want to be
With them. In them

We must be prepared
To embrace peace
That instant
That very moment

We have to be
Convinced
Otherwise it won't
Happen

Preparing the mind
Is the pertinent part
Determination for it
The second important

So peace and happiness
Are there for us
Just that we should be
Sure and persuasive

With our own self
Want it at all costs
Desire it dearly
And be determined

When we're convinced
When we're determined
It's easy to find peace
Nothing can perturb us

Nothing can stop us
From everlasting happiness

Paridhei 🙏 🖤

94

WE WILL NEED...

We will need
To know the real truth
We will need
To get the clear meaning

Of things around us
Of events, happenings
Of people, their intentions
Of situations, circumstances

We will need critical thinking
To solve problems
To find solutions
To take the correct action

We will need intuition
To find the right path
Amongst jumbled up paths
Find a way through mayhem

We will need to control
Unchecked emotions, feelings
Which will create chaos
Confusion and turmoil

Anger, hatered, jealousy
Fear, sadness, inferiority
All of these
Need to be kept at bay

We will need to put a check
On negativity which
Gives rise to stress, anxiety
Depression and melancholy

We will need super intelligence
Unlimited creativity
Sharp decision making
To get ahead in life

So many teachers
Gurus and saints
Have come and gone
And still living

Have taught us
That meditation
Holds the key
To all these problems

Meditate meditate
Meditate meditate
Let's find time in our life
To just sit and meditate

Paridhei 🙏 ♥

95

WHAT ARE WE LOOKING FOR

What truth are we looking for
What more are we seeking

Don't we have enough
We need
To do the work

The quest is going to be
Never ending
If we only keep
Searching

Let's keep our eyes
At the task
To the divine
To the guru
To the masters

Our hearts
Our minds
Our soul
Reaching
Up to them

We'll get whatever it takes
We'll know what is required

Just keep doing the work
Keep working
Keep contributing

Truth will reveal itself
Things will happen
When we're ready for it
We will get whatever
Is required
When we need it

All we need to ask for
Is being better instruments

We need to do what
Our potential is
And keep stretching
A little bit more
A little better than before

We will get the blessings
We will get the help
We will get the skill
We will get the knowledge
We will get the power

All of it
When it's needed

By just keeping
On working

We will see
We will blossom
When the time comes

Paridhei 🙏 🖤

96

WHAT WE THINK WE BECOME

We are taught
To be so
Careful of what
We eat and drink
What we consume
From our mouth

We're so bothered
By our looks
Our appearance
Our external
Demeanour
All that's outside

We concentrate on
Our physical efforts
The hard work
We put in
On the outside
What we do externally

But hardly anyone
Is talking about
What we feed
Our mind
What thoughts
We are thinking

When the truth is
Everything is in
The mind
Everything depends
What's happening
In there

If we have this
One element
Under control
We will win
Big wars
Happening outside

Our mind
And thoughts
Determine even our
Physical health
Not only
Mental health

Our body becomes
What our mind
Feeds it
Whatever web
Our mind spins
Body is caught in it

Even our material
Success and gains
Are all dependent
On the mind
And thoughts
What we think

Think positive
Our mind and body
Will be healthy
Don't think negative
We will keep
Illness at bay

Abundance thoughts
Success thoughts
Triumphant thoughts
Will get abundance
Success and prosperity
In all areas of our life

It's an internal job
It's all about
What we are inside
In our heads
In our minds
In our thoughts

What we think
We become
Physically
Mentally
Materially
Externally

We are a
By product
Of our mind
Our persona
Takes shape
Of what's inside

Paridhei 🙏 🖤

A pranic healer's view

97

WHEN I WILL

When i will
Be more capable
Then i will
Do service

When i will
Know more
Then i will
Teach others

When i will
Be more
Accomplished
I will heal others

When i will
Be more evolved
Then i will
Help others evolve

These are
The limiting
Beliefs
We all have

Our guru
Taught us
Gave us
Confidence

That we can
Do it now
Right away
Whatever our state

We don't need
To wait
To do service
To help others

We don't need
To delay
Healing others
Evolving others

Just plunge
Go and serve
Go and heal
Go and help

Go and teach
Go and be a part
Of the evolution
Of humanity

Only by actively
Participating
Being a part of
The process

Will we also
Evolve
And progress
And grow

When we teach
We will learn
Better and more
We will be wiser

When we empower
Others
We will gain
More power

The more
We use our
Mind and heart
Actions for good

The good we
Do and spread
We occupy
Ourselves with

Will attract
Goodness to us
Will attract
Greatness to us

We don't have
To be perfect
We should be
Willing to serve

That's all

Paridhei 🙏 ♥

Dedicated to my guru
Master Choa Kok Sui
And his teachings.
And his blessings.
And his empowerment to us.

WHO AM I TO JUDGE YOU?

Whenever we're
Criticising people
Just stop
Say to yourself
Who am i to judge you

Whenever we're
Disliking people
Just stop
Say to yourself
Who am i to judge you

Whenever people
Wrong us
We do feel the urge
To lash out at them
Just stop
Say to yourself
Who am i to judge you

Whenever we have
The urge to be jealous
And despise someone
Just stop
Say to yourself
Who am i to judge you

Want to be peaceful
Want to be happy
Want to increase your output
Want to be more productive
Want to be more successful

Just don't judge
No matter what

Paridhei 🙏 🖤

99

WHOLESOME THOUGHTS

Yes, it's difficult
To get rid of thoughts
They're always
Cropping up
Being produced
As if in a factory
Churning out
One after another

When it's difficult
To steer clear
Of them, then
Why not think
Meaningful
Purposeful
Thoughts
Positive thoughts

When our mind
Is anyways going
To be involved
In mental activity
Ambitions, planning
Problems, solutions
Activity for
Material gains

Why not have
Noble goals too
Virtuous gains
And plan and aim
For such lofty
Ideas, aims
And ambitions
Aim higher

Occupy our mind
With planning
Preparation
Organisation
Design, create
For higher purpose
For elevated advantages

We all must know
The importance of
Reaching for
Spiritual growth
Inner elevation
Evolution of the soul
True advancement
Genuine progress

No profit we get
In the ordinary
Can match these
Gifts and achievements
That lead us to
An advantage
A superior reward
A better us

So think
Wholesome thoughts
Then it won't
Matter much
Whether they
Go away or not
Soon we will
Find peace, tranquility

Aim extraordinary
And we will be
Truly happy and
Blessed forever
No one and nothing
Not even this life
Can take away
These precious gains

Paridhei 🙏 🖤

100

WHY ARE WE HERE?

Between our
Hectic schedules
Our busy days
Amidst the hustle bustle
Let's take some time off
Sit quietly, contemplate

And meditate on
Why are we here ?
What's our purpose ?
Know the deeper
Meaning of
Our life, our existence

Just living unaware
In ignorance
Senselessly running after
Material things
Satisfying our wants
Succumbing to our ego

Is such a waste of time
Waste of a priceless life,
If we have not found
Our true purpose

The real reason
We're here, why we live

Our main purpose
Is to be happy
And peaceful beings
To affect the world
With our peace and cheer
To make it a better place

To evolve ourselves
Help the world evolve
Only running after
Material things
Is not going to
Get us there

If we are not happy
We will create unhappy
Ripples all around us
No matter what we achieve
We will disturb the world
Create turmoil and chaos

True happiness
Will not be found
In just amassing wealth
Or only aiming for worldly
Success and recognition
Always being in a scurry

We got to take out time
To do self introspection
To improve ourselves
To meditate
To do service
To help and bless

Only truly knowing
Ourselves and others
Trying to make
Ourselves better
Helping others also uplift
Getting healed and heal

Will get us elation and peace
And make us shine
Only lighting ourselves up
Can we light the world
And make it shine too
Impact it with positivity

Let's heal ourselves, the world
Make it a better place
For everyone
Not just for us
True exhilaration delight
And glee will be ours

Paridhei

101

WITH A THOUGHT

Everything develops
With a thought

Everything starts
With a strong will

Everything begins
With a firm resolve

Everything will elaborate
On our vision

It's all in the mind
It all starts there

The stronger our thought
Our will, our resolve

The faster we will
Reach our goals

The faster we will
Manifest our dreams

So, it all depends
On the strength of these

But, if there's chaos, turmoil,
Negativity in the mind

Will we be able to
Produce strong thoughts?

Will we be able to get the
Razor sharp thinking ?

Will we get the clarity?
Will we get the answers?

Here, we see the need to purify
Our minds and thoughts

We see need to steer clear
Of negative thoughts

It's pertinent to introspect
It's important to purify

Only pure and positive thoughts,
Emotions and feelings

Will lead us to success
Will reach us to our goals

Will take us to greater heights
Will bring us to happiness

Paridhei 🙏 ♥

BIO

Sqn Ldr Paridhei Singh Karthik (Retd.) is a retired pilot from the Indian Airforce with 2500 hours of flying, was cleared for various transport operational roles.

She's a multifaceted personality, a sports person with participation in national level basketball and judo. Also an adventure sportsperson she has national and international level skiing, white water rafting and skydiving, participation. She has Rafted various major rivers of india.

She is the founder and president of Indian Federation of Adventure Sports and Racing, which is affiliated to World Obstacle Federation.

She's a Kathak dancer. A yoga teacher, a Pranic Healer, and Arhatic Yogi. Regular practitioner of Meditation and Yoga.

She's a motivational and inspirational speaker; A coach and a trainer.

She does service through IFASR and her NGO- Hamara Sansar, Rotary and Pranichealing.

She has always been interested in philosophy and spirituality and that motivated her to take up PranicHealing and Arhatic Yoga.

She likes to be known as a student of life and a traveller.

Photographs of the author in uniform, with aircraft.

Photograph of the author in one of her adventure escapades: Skiing.

Photograph of the author performing on stage, The Indian Classical Dance Form: Kathak

www.ingramcontent.com/pod-product-compliance
Lightning Source LLC
LaVergne TN
LVHW041906070526
838199LV00051BA/2520